Charles Lindbergh

SADDLEBACK
EDUCATIONAL PUBLISHING

Saddleback's Graphic Biographies

SADDLEBACK
EDUCATIONAL PUBLISHING
Three Watson
Irvine, CA 92618-2767
Website: www.sdlback.com

ISBN-13: 978-1-59905-218-2
ISBN-10: 1-59905-218-0
eBook: 978-1-60291-581-7

Printed in China

Charles Augustus Lindbergh was a pioneer of the air. He was the first man to fly non-stop across the Atlantic Ocean. He took off from New York at dawn on May 20, 1927, and landed in Paris 33 and one-half hours later.

"Lucky Lindy" and the "Lone Eagle" was what they called him when he returned to New York. Millions of people turned out to welcome him. He was hardly more than a boy, but his daring flight made him a world hero. He was the father of modern aviation.

He was born in Detroit on February 4, 1902, the son of Charles Augustus Lindbergh and Eva Land.

But he grew up in Little Falls, Minnesota, where Pike Creek flows into the Mississippi River.

He lived there with his mother for most of every year.

Thank you, Charles.

My pleasure, Mother.

Each fall they traveled to Washington, D.C., to spend the winter with Charles' father. He was one of Minnesota's representatives to the U.S. Congress.

And each spring ...

Oh boy! It's back to the farm.

Yes, its home to Minnesota.

But the happiest of days was when Charles would hear his father's special whistle.

Come on, Wahgoosh! That's Dad's whippoorwill* call. That means he's back home!

Oh boy, you're home.

Then summer had really arrived.

Look at that bird take off!

*a nocturnal bird with a loud repeated call suggestive of its name

The summer Charles was ten, his father arrived with a surprise.

Wow, I can't believe it. Dad has a car!

That summer with his father at the wheel, Charles rode on the running boards of the car.

This is much more fun than riding inside!

And when his father went to Washington that fall, Charles taught himself to drive.

Now you be careful, Charles!

I will, Mother.

Soon he was driving his mother everywhere.

I'm so glad you learned to drive, Charles. This is most helpful.

In the summer of 1913, Charles' father came home to campaign for the 1914 election. Charles was waiting at the depot.

Young Charles drove the car here?

What a surprise!

Mom said that I could drive around with you this summer.

I don't see why not, you're better at this than I am.

This motor is easy to work on.

It was a fun summer. Young Charles was too busy tinkering with the engine to listen to speeches or worry about politics.

In the summer of 1915, Congressman Lindbergh was asked to explore the headwaters of the Mississippi River.

They've asked me to lead a two-man expedition up the river.

Who's the second man?

You are!

The voyage was an important experience for young Charles. For six weeks they traveled in the wild. They hunted and fished for their food.

This is the way Robinson Crusoe lived.

Yes! I like to hunt and fish for our food.

They visited the Chippewa Indians.

You are now brothers of the Chippewa tribe.

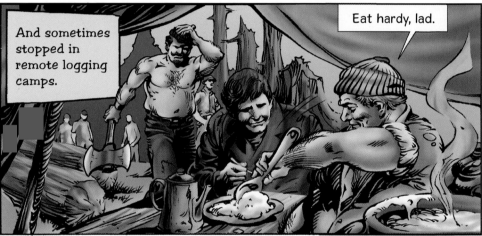

And sometimes stopped in remote logging camps.

Eat hardy, lad.

The next summer the Lindberghs bought a new car, and Charles drove his father around while he campaigned for the U.S. Senate

VOTE FOR LINDBERGH!

Charles' father lost the election. This was the end of his career as a congressman in Washington.

That fall his father went back to Washington, D.C., for one last winter. But Mrs. Lindbergh had other plans.

I'll be done rebuilding this motor in two days, Mother.

Wonderful, this trip to California will do us both good.

They hoped to arrive in ten days, but the roads in those days were very bad.

I think we have enough gas to make it to the next town.

After forty days they reached the coast.

We made it!

I think we should stay for the winter.

When they went back to Minnesota, his parents decided not to live together anymore. The First World War was coming, and Charles' father started to make plans for the future.

You'll be the man in the family now. It will be hard to get food. I think you'd better run the farm.

Yes, yes!

The farm became his life. At sixteen he was an experienced farmer who rose everyday before dawn.

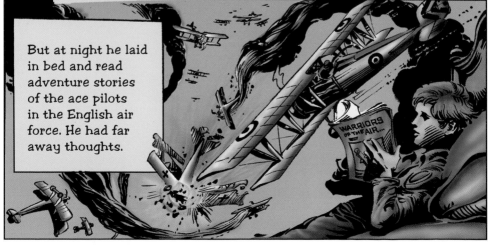

But at night he laid in bed and read adventure stories of the ace pilots in the English air force. He had far away thoughts.

WARRIORS OF THE AIR...

He planned to join the Army Air Corps as soon as he was old enough. But the war ended, and his mother had other plans.

Thank goodness, now that the war's over you don't have to grow our food. You can go to college now.

But at college Charles spent more time riding his motorcycle than studying.

You'd be in trouble if your brakes failed going down this hill.

I'll bet I can make the turn at the bottom without using the brakes.

Don't be a fool. You'll be killed.

But the young daredevil gave it a try.

Luckily, no bones were broken.

You know, I could do it if I gun the motor just as I make the turn.

Sure enough, he gave it another try.

He made it!

He's almost flying!

But that wasn't enough.

NEBRASKA AIRCRAFT COMPANY

I've dropped out of college with my life savings. I want to learn to fly.

Well I think we can get you started.

Soon he was on his way to being a pilot.

Nice landing, Slim.

In those days barnstorming* was just about the only work a young pilot could find.

STATE FAIR

* to pilot one's airplane in exhibition stunts

But it was dangerous and the life was hard.

There were many times when he slept on the ground beside his plane.

So on March 15, 1924, young Lindbergh joined the Army Air Corps at Brooks Field in Texas.

You'll learn a lot here, Cadet Lindbergh.

Yes, sir!

A year later he graduated first in his class.

Congratulations, Lieutenant Lindbergh.

Thank you, sir.

Then young Lindbergh went to St. Louis hoping to teach flying, but something happened that he didn't expect.

We like your reputation, Slim. We want you to be chief pilot on the new St. Louis to Chicago air mail run.

On April 26, 1926, he made the first air mail flight between St. Louis and Chicago.

Congratulations, Slim, you made it in only four hours.

That summer Lindbergh made most of his flights on time. When fall came, so did bad weather.

Once he had to parachute in when he could not find a place to land.

But with the help of a friendly farmer, he got his mail bag quickly to a train.

Thank you.

Good luck, Slim.

These were the exciting early years of flying. Charles Lindbergh had big dreams.

Suppose I fly a plane with special tanks for extra gasoline.

I could fly all night by the moon. I could even fly from New York to Paris.

Then Lindbergh found out that a prize of $25,000 had been offered for the first plane to fly non-stop from New York to Paris. But he needed help to get ready for the trip. He asked some businessmen for money to help him buy his airplane.

You all have money and love this city, St. Louis. Why not help me buy a plane? We'll call it the *Spirit of St. Louis*. If I succeed the name of the city you love will be on the lips of everyone in the world.

It worked, soon he had enough money.

But finding the right plane wasn't so easy.

Will you sell me that Wright-Bellanca for my flight?

Never! It would be impossible to cross the ocean in a single engine plane.

Several companies turned him down, but Lindbergh was determined.

I'm going to San Diego, California. The Ryan Aircraft Company says they can build me a plane in sixty days.

Better hurry, Slim. Other flyers are getting ready too.

By chance, Lindbergh had found a small group of expert engineers and craftsmen.

I just hope we can get her in the air in time.

If we don't, it won't be your fault. Your men are working day and night.

On April 28, 1927, Lindbergh piloted the *Spirit of St. Louis* onto the runway for the first time.

On May 10, 1927, Lindbergh made a record flight from San Diego to St. Louis to say farewell to his backers.

She's a good ship. I know we can do it.

Two other planes were already in New York waiting to take off. Lindbergh flew there as quickly as he could.

For days clouds and rain kept everyone grounded.

Well, if I can't take off, nobody else can either.

But then reports arrived that the weather over the ocean was clearing.

Good news! I'll go at dawn.

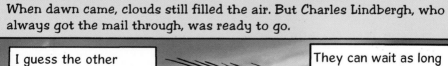

When dawn came, clouds still filled the air. But Charles Lindbergh, who always got the mail through, was ready to go.

I guess the other flyers must be waiting for a sunny day to fly across the Atlantic.

They can wait as long as they want, but I'm going. I want to be first.

The great moment had come. Loaded with 400 gallons of gasoline, the heavy plane splashed down the runway.

He barely cleared the telephone wires and trees at the end of the runway. At 7:54 a.m. on May 20, 1927, the *Spirit of St. Louis* was headed for Paris.

To save weight, Lindbergh had no radio on board. He would find his way by compass and by the stars.

That day he flew very low. Often he could see dolphins leaping over the waves.

As he went north, he flew over the iceberg-covered North Atlantic. It was freezing cold.

That night the moon rose, and he flew through clouds that were lit up like magnificent mountains.

He grew tired. Again and again he caught himself falling asleep. He knew that if he fell asleep, the plane would fall into the ocean.

About 4 o'clock the next afternoon, he flew over the Irish coast.

Soon the whole world knew.

Hurray!

Lindbergh has been seen over Ireland.

Three cheers! Three cheers for Charles Lindbergh!

Night had fallen, and it was dark when he spotted the lights of the Eiffel Tower in Paris, France. Then he began to look for Le Bourget Airport.

It seemed as if all of Paris was there to welcome him.

Hundreds of cars had parked along the runway to light the field, so that he could land safely.

He had flown from New York to Paris in 33 and one-half hours.

Charles Lindbergh was about to find out what it was like to be the most famous man in the world.

Lindbergh received honors from the President of France and King George V of England. Then President Coolidge sent a ship to bring him and his plane, the *Spirit of St. Louis,* back to America.

OUR LINDY

Back in American waters, they sailed into port. They were welcomed by a committee of four destroyers, two army blimps, and forty airplanes.

President Coolidge had brought Charles Lindbergh's mother to Washington, D.C., for the homecoming. The welcome was a grand one.

The entire country is proud of you, young man.

In the summer of 1927, Lindbergh made an air tour of the United States.

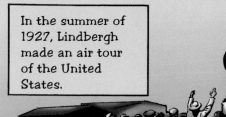

He flew 22,350 miles, led parades in 82 cities, and stayed at least one night in every state in the country. He wanted to prove that the air age had arrived.

That fall he made the first non-stop flight from Washington, D.C., to Mexico City.

He stayed with the U.S. Ambassador, Dwight Morrow, and his family.

There he met their daughter, Anne. A year and a half later they were married.

I think you and my daughter Anne will enjoy talking. Both of you have a strong interest in nature.

Together, with Anne as his navigator and radio operator, the Lindberghs toured the world in the air. They made many daring and record-breaking flights.

But a great tragedy happened. In 1931 their son Charles Augustus Lindbergh III was kidnapped and murdered.

LINDBERGH-BABY DEAD!

For many months there were headlines in the newspapers. Charles and Anne were unhappy about this. They wished to forget, but headlines sell papers.

In his later years Charles Lindbergh devoted his life to the causes of ecology and to protecting endangered* species of birds and animals.

In the Philippines, he worked with President Marcos to save a rare species of eagle.

During his final days, Charles Lindbergh lived on the island of Maui in Hawaii. He and Anne had built a simple house without electricity or air conditioning. There they lived, returning to closeness with nature and the wilderness, which was what they had come to value most.

THE END

* anyone or anything whose continued existence is threatened

Saddleback's Graphic Fiction & Nonfiction

If you enjoyed this Graphic Biography ... you will also enjoy our other graphic titles including:

Graphic Classics

- Around the World in Eighty Days
- The Best of Poe
- Black Beauty
- The Call of the Wild
- A Christmas Carol
- A Connecticut Yankee in King Arthur's Court
- Dr. Jekyll and Mr. Hyde
- Dracula
- Frankenstein
- The Great Adventures of Sherlock Holmes
- Gulliver's Travels
- Huckleberry Finn
- The Hunchback of Notre Dame
- The Invisible Man
- Jane Eyre
- Journey to the Center of the Earth
- Kidnapped
- The Last of the Mohicans
- The Man in the Iron Mask
- Moby Dick
- The Mutiny On Board H.M.S. Bounty
- The Mysterious Island
- The Prince and the Pauper
- The Red Badge of Courage
- The Scarlet Letter
- The Swiss Family Robinson
- A Tale of Two Cities
- The Three Musketeers
- The Time Machine
- Tom Sawyer
- Treasure Island
- 20,000 Leagues Under the Sea
- The War of the Worlds

Graphic Shakespeare

- As You Like It
- Hamlet
- Julius Caesar
- King Lear
- Macbeth
- The Merchant of Venice
- A Midsummer Night's Dream
- Othello
- Romeo and Juliet
- The Taming of the Shrew
- The Tempest
- Twelfth Night

SADDLEBACK
EDUCATIONAL PUBLISHING